# Table of Contents

Preface .................................................................................................. 6

**Chapter 1: Introduction to Car Auctions** ......................................................... 7

   1.1 What are Car Auctions? ..................................................................... 7

   1.2 Types of Car Auctions ....................................................................... 7

      1.2.1 Physical Auctions ..................................................................... 7

      1.2.2 Online Auctions ....................................................................... 7

      1.2.3 Government Auctions .............................................................. 7

      1.2.4 Dealer Auctions ....................................................................... 8

      1.2.5 Salvage Auctions ..................................................................... 8

   1.3 Benefits of Buying Cars at Auctions ................................................... 8

      1.3.1 Competitive Prices ................................................................... 8

      1.3.2 Variety of Options .................................................................... 8

      1.3.3 Fast Transactions .................................................................... 8

      1.3.4 Unique Buying Experience ....................................................... 8

      1.3.5 Transparency .......................................................................... 8

      1.3.6 Accessibility ............................................................................ 8

      1.3.7 Opportunity for Profit ............................................................... 9

**Chapter 2: Overview of the Malaysian Car Auction Market** ............................. 10

   2.1 History and Evolution of Car Auctions in Malaysia ............................. 10

   2.2 Major Players in the Market .............................................................. 10

      2.2.1 Government Agencies ............................................................ 10

      2.2.2 Private Auction Houses .......................................................... 10

      2.2.3 Online Platforms .................................................................... 10

      2.2.4 Dealer Auctions ..................................................................... 11

   2.3 Trends and Growth Opportunities ..................................................... 11

      2.3.1 Digital Transformation ............................................................ 11

      2.3.2 Increased Transparency ........................................................ 11

- 2.3.3 Diversification of Inventory ............... 11
- 2.3.4 Emphasis on Compliance and Regulation ............... 11
- Chapter 3: Understanding the Auction Process ............... 12
  - 3.1 Pre-Auction Preparations ............... 12
    - 3.1.1 Registration ............... 12
    - 3.1.2 Research ............... 12
    - 3.1.3 Budgeting ............... 12
    - 3.1.4 Inspection ............... 12
  - 3.2 Bidding Process ............... 12
    - 3.2.1 Auction Format ............... 13
    - 3.2.2 Bidding Strategies ............... 13
    - 3.2.3 Live Bidding ............... 13
    - 3.2.4 Online Bidding ............... 13
  - 3.3 Payment and Ownership Transfer Procedures ............... 13
    - 3.3.1 Payment ............... 13
    - 3.3.2 Documentation ............... 13
    - 3.3.3 Vehicle Pickup or Delivery ............... 13
- Chapter 4: Types of Cars Available at Auctions ............... 15
  - 4.1 New vs. Used Cars ............... 15
    - 4.1.1 New Cars ............... 15
    - 4.1.2 Used Cars ............... 15
  - 4.2 Different Makes and Models ............... 15
    - 4.2.1 Mainstream Brands ............... 15
    - 4.2.2 Luxury Brands ............... 15
    - 4.2.3 Specialty Vehicles ............... 16
  - 4.3 Factors Affecting Availability and Pricing ............... 16
    - 4.3.1 Condition ............... 16
    - 4.3.2 Market Demand ............... 16
    - 4.3.3 Auction Timing ............... 16

## Chapter 5: Tips for Successful Bidding ................................................................ 17
### 5.1 Research Before Bidding ........................................................................ 17
#### 5.1.1 Understanding Market Value ............................................................ 17
#### 5.1.2 Vehicle History ................................................................................ 17
#### 5.1.3 Inspection ...................................................................................... 17
### 5.2 Set a Budget and Stick to It ..................................................................... 17
### 5.3 Be Strategic in Your Bidding .................................................................... 17
#### 5.3.1 Start Slowly .................................................................................... 18
#### 5.3.2 Bid Confidently ............................................................................... 18
#### 5.3.3 Know When to Stop ........................................................................ 18
### 5.4 Attend Multiple Auctions .......................................................................... 18
### 5.5 Learn from Experience ............................................................................ 18
## Chapter 6: Legal and Financial Considerations ..................................................... 19
### 6.1 Legal Requirements ............................................................................... 19
#### 6.1.1 Ownership Transfer ........................................................................ 19
#### 6.1.2 Title Checks .................................................................................... 19
#### 6.1.3 Registration and Taxes ................................................................... 19
### 6.2 Financial Considerations ........................................................................ 19
#### 6.2.1 Buyer's Premium ............................................................................ 19
#### 6.2.2 Taxes and Duties ............................................................................ 20
#### 6.2.3 Financing Options .......................................................................... 20
### 6.3 Legal Protections ................................................................................... 20
#### 6.3.1 Auction Terms and Conditions ........................................................ 20
#### 6.3.2 Warranty and Guarantees ............................................................... 20
#### 6.3.3 Dispute Resolution ......................................................................... 20
## Chapter 7: Risks and Pitfalls to Avoid .................................................................... 21
### 7.1 Hidden Costs .......................................................................................... 21
#### 7.1.1 Buyer's Premium ............................................................................ 21
#### 7.1.2 Taxes and Duties ............................................................................ 21

- 7.1.3 Inspection and Repairs ................................................................. 21
- 7.2 Quality Issues .................................................................................... 21
  - 7.2.1 Mechanical Problems ................................................................. 22
  - 7.2.2 Cosmetic Damage ...................................................................... 22
  - 7.2.3 Salvage Title ................................................................................ 22
- 7.3 Avoiding Scams and Fraud ................................................................ 22
  - 7.3.1 Verify Seller Credentials ............................................................ 22
  - 7.3.2 Check Vehicle History ............................................................... 22
  - 7.3.3 Beware of Unrealistic Deals ...................................................... 22
- 7.4 Lack of Warranty or Recourse .......................................................... 23
  - 7.4.1 Inspect Vehicles Thoroughly .................................................... 23
  - 7.4.2 Consider Professional Inspection ............................................ 23
  - 7.4.3 Know Your Rights ..................................................................... 23

## Chapter 8: Case Studies and Success Stories .................................... 24
- 8.1 Case Study: Adam's Auction Adventure .......................................... 24
- 8.2 Success Story: Sarah's Smart Investment ........................................ 24

## Chapter 9: Future Outlook and Trends ............................................... 26
- 9.1 Emerging Technologies .................................................................... 26
  - 9.1.1 Online Auction Platforms ......................................................... 26
  - 9.1.2 Artificial Intelligence and Data Analytics ............................... 26
  - 9.1.3 Virtual Reality and Augmented Reality ................................... 26
- 9.2 Sustainable Practices ........................................................................ 26
  - 9.2.1 Electric and Hybrid Vehicles ..................................................... 26
  - 9.2.2 Green Initiatives ......................................................................... 27
  - 9.2.3 Emission Standards Compliance .............................................. 27
- 9.3 Shift in Consumer Preferences ........................................................ 27
  - 9.3.1 Demand for Connected Cars .................................................... 27
  - 9.3.2 Flexible Ownership Models ...................................................... 27
  - 9.3.3 Online Participation ................................................................... 27

## 9.4 Market Expansion .................................................................... 28
### 9.4.1 Regional Integration ........................................................ 28
### 9.4.2 Digital Transformation .................................................... 28
### 9.4.3 Diversity of Inventory ..................................................... 28
## Chapter 10: Additional Resources and Glossary ..................................... 29
### 10.1 Additional Resources ........................................................ 29
#### 10.1.1 Online Auction Platforms ............................................ 29
#### 10.1.2 Auction Houses ........................................................... 29
#### 10.1.3 Automotive Forums and Communities ..................... 29
#### 10.1.4 Automotive Publications ............................................ 30
#### 10.1.5 Government Websites ............................................... 30
### 10.2 Glossary of Auction Terms ................................................ 30
## Frequently Asked Questions (FAQ) ........................................................ 33

# Preface

Welcome to the exciting world of car auctions in Malaysia! Whether you're a seasoned automotive enthusiast or a curious first-time bidder, this ebook is your comprehensive guide to navigating the dynamic and fast-paced landscape of automotive auctions in Malaysia.

Car auctions offer a unique and thrilling marketplace where buyers and sellers come together to buy and sell vehicles of all types, from economy cars to luxury models, at competitive prices. With the rise of online platforms and the expansion of auction houses across the country, car auctions have become more accessible and diverse than ever before.

In this ebook, we'll take you on a journey through the ins and outs of car auctions in Malaysia, providing you with valuable insights, practical tips, and expert advice to help you make informed decisions and achieve success in your auction pursuits. From understanding the auction process and bidding strategies to navigating legal and financial considerations, we'll cover everything you need to know to participate confidently in car auctions.

Through real-life case studies, success stories, and in-depth analysis, we'll explore the diverse opportunities and challenges of buying and selling vehicles at auction. Whether you're searching for your dream car, looking for a bargain, or seeking to expand your automotive business, car auctions offer a wealth of options and possibilities for every buyer and seller.

As the automotive industry evolves and technology continues to transform the auction market, it's essential to stay informed and adaptable. By equipping yourself with the knowledge and resources provided in this ebook, you'll be well-prepared to navigate the ever-changing landscape of automotive auctions and seize opportunities for success.

Whether you're a seasoned auction veteran or a newcomer exploring the world of car auctions for the first time, I invite you to join us on this exciting journey. Together, let's embark on an adventure into the thrilling world of automotive auctions in Malaysia!

Happy bidding!

**LIM KAM THIM**
March 2024

# Chapter 1: Introduction to Car Auctions

Welcome to the world of car auctions, where enthusiasts and bargain hunters alike converge to find their dream vehicles at competitive prices. In this chapter, we'll delve into the fundamentals of car auctions, exploring what they are, the various types available, and the advantages they offer to buyers.

## 1.1 What are Car Auctions?

Car auctions are events or platforms where vehicles are sold to the highest bidder. Unlike traditional car dealerships, where prices are set, auctions allow buyers to determine the value of a vehicle through competitive bidding. Auctions can take place in physical locations, such as auction houses or open lots, or they can be conducted online through specialized websites and platforms.

## 1.2 Types of Car Auctions

There are several types of car auctions, each catering to different audiences and purposes:

### 1.2.1 Physical Auctions
These are traditional auctions where buyers gather at a specific location to bid on vehicles displayed on-site. Physical auctions offer the excitement of live bidding and the opportunity to inspect vehicles in person.

### 1.2.2 Online Auctions
With the advent of technology, online auctions have become increasingly popular. Buyers can participate in auctions remotely, bidding on vehicles through websites or dedicated auction platforms. Online auctions provide convenience and access to a wider range of vehicles.

### 1.2.3 Government Auctions
Government agencies often auction off surplus vehicles, seized cars, or fleet vehicles that are no longer needed. These auctions can offer great deals on well-maintained vehicles, but buyers should be aware of any restrictions or special requirements.

### 1.2.4 Dealer Auctions
Some auctions are exclusive to licensed dealers, allowing them to acquire inventory for their dealership businesses. While these auctions may not be accessible to individual buyers, they play a significant role in the automotive industry.

### 1.2.5 Salvage Auctions
Salvage auctions specialize in selling vehicles that have been damaged or declared total losses by insurance companies. These auctions attract buyers looking for project cars or spare parts.

## 1.3 Benefits of Buying Cars at Auctions

Participating in car auctions offers several advantages for buyers:

### 1.3.1 Competitive Prices
Vehicles at auctions often sell for below market value, allowing buyers to find great deals and potential bargains.

### 1.3.2 Variety of Options
Auctions feature a diverse selection of vehicles, ranging from economy cars to luxury vehicles, and even rare or specialty models.

### 1.3.3 Fast Transactions
The auction process is designed for efficiency. Successful bidders can quickly finalize transactions, expediting the purchase and ownership transfer of the vehicle.

### 1.3.4 Unique Buying Experience
Participating in a car auction provides a unique and exhilarating buying experience. The competitive nature of bidding and the anticipation of winning contribute to the allure of auctions.

### 1.3.5 Transparency
Auctions typically provide detailed information about each vehicle, including its condition, mileage, and history, enabling buyers to make informed decisions.

### 1.3.6 Accessibility
With both physical and online auctions, buyers have the flexibility to participate from anywhere, making it convenient to find and purchase their desired vehicles.

**1.3.7 Opportunity for Profit**
Some buyers purchase vehicles at auctions for resale, either as-is or after refurbishment, potentially earning a profit from the transaction.

In the subsequent chapters of this ebook, we'll explore the intricacies of the car auction process in Malaysia, providing you with the knowledge and tools to navigate the exciting world of automotive auctions with confidence. So buckle up and get ready to embark on your auction adventure!

# Chapter 2: Overview of the Malaysian Car Auction Market

In this chapter, we'll take a closer look at the landscape of car auctions in Malaysia, including their history, key players, and current trends shaping the market.

## 2.1 History and Evolution of Car Auctions in Malaysia

The concept of car auctions in Malaysia traces back several decades, with the market evolving over time to meet the changing needs of consumers and the automotive industry. Initially, car auctions were primarily conducted by government agencies, such as the Royal Malaysian Customs Department and the Road Transport Department (JPJ), to auction off seized or impounded vehicles. However, in recent years, the market has expanded to include private auction houses, online platforms, and dealer auctions, catering to a broader range of buyers and sellers.

## 2.2 Major Players in the Market

Several entities play significant roles in the Malaysian car auction market:

### 2.2.1 Government Agencies
The Royal Malaysian Customs Department and JPJ continue to hold regular auctions for seized vehicles, providing opportunities for buyers to acquire vehicles at competitive prices.

### 2.2.2 Private Auction Houses
Numerous private auction houses operate in Malaysia, organizing auctions for both used and repossessed vehicles. These auction houses often specialize in specific vehicle categories or serve niche markets, such as luxury cars or commercial vehicles.

### 2.2.3 Online Platforms
With the growing popularity of e-commerce, online auction platforms have emerged as a convenient way for buyers to participate in auctions from the comfort of their homes. Websites and mobile apps offer a wide selection of vehicles and streamlined bidding processes.

### 2.2.4 Dealer Auctions
Licensed dealerships also conduct auctions to acquire inventory for their businesses. These auctions may feature trade-in vehicles, lease returns, or surplus stock, providing dealers with access to a diverse range of vehicles.

## 2.3 Trends and Growth Opportunities

The Malaysian car auction market continues to evolve, driven by various trends and opportunities:

### 2.3.1 Digital Transformation
The shift towards online auctions has accelerated, with more buyers and sellers embracing digital platforms for their convenience and accessibility. Online auctions offer features such as live bidding, virtual inspections, and secure payment options.

### 2.3.2 Increased Transparency
Auction houses and online platforms are enhancing transparency by providing detailed vehicle information, including condition reports, service histories, and vehicle identification numbers (VINs). This transparency builds trust and confidence among buyers, reducing the risk of purchasing undisclosed issues.

### 2.3.3 Diversification of Inventory
Auctions are offering a broader range of vehicles, including electric and hybrid models, as well as specialized vehicles for commercial and recreational purposes. This diversification caters to the evolving needs and preferences of buyers in the market.

### 2.3.4 Emphasis on Compliance and Regulation
With the growing emphasis on consumer protection and regulatory compliance, auction houses are implementing measures to ensure that vehicles sold meet legal and safety requirements. This includes verifying vehicle ownership, conducting inspections, and facilitating proper documentation for buyers.

As the Malaysian car auction market continues to mature, opportunities abound for buyers to find their ideal vehicles and for sellers to reach a wider audience.

# Chapter 3: Understanding the Auction Process

In this chapter, we'll delve into the intricacies of the car auction process in Malaysia, guiding you through the steps involved from pre-auction preparations to completing a successful purchase.

## 3.1 Pre-Auction Preparations

Before participating in a car auction, it's essential to prepare adequately to ensure a smooth and successful experience:

### 3.1.1 Registration
Most auctions require buyers to register in advance, either online or in person. Registration typically involves providing personal information, such as identification documents and contact details, and agreeing to the auction terms and conditions.

### 3.1.2 Research
Conduct thorough research on the vehicles available at the auction, including their make, model, year, and estimated market value. Review vehicle histories, such as accident reports and service records, to assess their condition and potential resale value.

### 3.1.3 Budgeting
Set a realistic budget for your auction purchases, taking into account the cost of the vehicle, buyer's fees, taxes, and any additional expenses, such as transportation and repairs. Stick to your budget to avoid overspending and financial strain.

### 3.1.4 Inspection
Whenever possible, inspect the vehicles you're interested in before the auction begins. Check for signs of damage, wear and tear, mechanical issues, and inconsistencies in the vehicle's condition. Bring along a trusted mechanic or knowledgeable friend to assist you in the inspection process.

## 3.2 Bidding Process

The bidding process is the heart of any car auction, where buyers compete to secure their desired vehicles:

### 3.2.1 Auction Format
Auctions may follow different formats, such as open bidding, sealed bidding, or proxy bidding. Familiarize yourself with the auction format and rules to understand how bidding will proceed.

### 3.2.2 Bidding Strategies
Develop effective bidding strategies based on your budget, the value of the vehicle, and the level of competition. Decide on your maximum bid and stick to it, avoiding emotional impulses that may lead to overbidding.

### 3.2.3 Live Bidding
In physical auctions, bidding occurs in real-time as auctioneers announce each vehicle and accept bids from the audience. Raise your hand or signal your bid to the auctioneer to participate in the bidding process.

### 3.2.4 Online Bidding
For online auctions, place your bids through the auction platform's website or mobile app. Monitor the bidding activity closely and submit your bids promptly to stay competitive.

## 3.3 Payment and Ownership Transfer Procedures

Once you've successfully won a vehicle at auction, it's time to complete the transaction and take ownership:

### 3.3.1 Payment
Follow the auction house's payment instructions to settle the purchase price, including any applicable taxes, fees, and buyer's premiums. Payment methods may include cash, certified checks, bank transfers, or credit cards.

### 3.3.2 Documentation
Obtain the necessary documentation to transfer ownership of the vehicle legally. This may include a bill of sale, transfer of ownership form, and vehicle registration documents. Ensure that all paperwork is completed accurately and signed by both parties.

### 3.3.3 Vehicle Pickup or Delivery
Arrange for the pickup or delivery of the vehicle according to the auction house's policies. Coordinate with transportation services or logistics providers to transport the vehicle to your desired location safely.

By understanding the auction process and following these steps diligently, you can navigate the complexities of car auctions in Malaysia with confidence and achieve your goals of acquiring quality vehicles at competitive prices.

# Chapter 4: Types of Cars Available at Auctions

In this chapter, we'll explore the diverse range of vehicles that are available at car auctions in Malaysia, from economy cars to luxury models, and everything in between. Understanding the types of cars available will help you identify the best options to suit your preferences, budget, and requirements.

## 4.1 New vs. Used Cars

Car auctions offer both new and used vehicles, catering to different buyer preferences and budgetary constraints:

### 4.1.1 New Cars
Some auctions feature brand-new vehicles that have never been driven or registered. These cars may come from dealership overstock, manufacturer surplus, or canceled orders. Buying a new car at auction can offer significant savings compared to purchasing from a dealership.

### 4.1.2 Used Cars
The majority of vehicles at auctions are used cars, ranging from lightly pre-owned models to older vehicles with higher mileage. Used cars may come from various sources, including trade-ins, lease returns, rental fleets, and repossessions. Buyers can find a wide selection of used cars at auctions, often at discounted prices compared to the retail market.

## 4.2 Different Makes and Models

Car auctions feature vehicles from various manufacturers, encompassing popular brands and lesser-known makes:

### 4.2.1 Mainstream Brands
Auctions typically offer a diverse selection of mainstream brands, such as Toyota, Honda, Nissan, and Proton. These brands are known for their reliability, affordability, and widespread availability, making them popular choices among buyers.

### 4.2.2 Luxury Brands
For buyers seeking premium and luxury vehicles, auctions often feature models from prestigious brands like BMW, Mercedes-Benz, Audi, and Lexus. Luxury cars at auction may include sedans, SUVs, coupes, and convertibles, offering advanced features and high-end amenities.

### 4.2.3 Specialty Vehicles

Some auctions specialize in rare or specialty vehicles, catering to collectors and enthusiasts. These auctions may feature classic cars, vintage models, sports cars, exotic imports, and modified vehicles. Specialty vehicles often command higher prices and attract buyers with specific interests and preferences.

## 4.3 Factors Affecting Availability and Pricing

Several factors influence the availability and pricing of cars at auctions:

### 4.3.1 Condition

The condition of a vehicle significantly impacts its availability and pricing at auction. Well-maintained cars with low mileage and minimal wear and tear tend to command higher prices and attract more buyers. Conversely, vehicles with mechanical issues, cosmetic damage, or significant wear may sell for lower prices or be less desirable to buyers.

### 4.3.2 Market Demand

The demand for specific makes, models, and vehicle types can fluctuate based on market trends, consumer preferences, and economic factors. Popular models with high demand may attract more bidders and sell for higher prices, while less popular models may sell for lower prices or remain unsold.

### 4.3.3 Auction Timing

The timing of auctions can also influence the availability and pricing of cars. Auctions held during peak seasons or special events may attract more sellers and buyers, resulting in increased competition and higher prices. Conversely, auctions held during slower periods or economic downturns may offer better deals for buyers.

By understanding the types of cars available at auctions and the factors that affect their availability and pricing, you can make informed decisions when participating in car auctions in Malaysia.

# Chapter 5: Tips for Successful Bidding

In this chapter, we'll discuss essential tips and strategies to help you navigate the bidding process effectively and increase your chances of securing the vehicles you desire at car auctions in Malaysia.

## 5.1 Research Before Bidding

Before participating in an auction, conduct thorough research on the vehicles you're interested in. This includes:

### 5.1.1 Understanding Market Value
Research the market value of the vehicles you're considering by comparing similar models' prices in the retail market. This will help you set realistic bidding limits and avoid overpaying.

### 5.1.2 Vehicle History
Obtain vehicle history reports, if available, to learn about the vehicle's past ownership, accident history, service records, and any outstanding recalls or issues. A comprehensive understanding of the vehicle's history will enable you to make informed decisions and avoid purchasing problematic vehicles.

### 5.1.3 Inspection
Whenever possible, inspect the vehicles in person or hire a qualified mechanic to assess their condition. Look for signs of damage, wear and tear, and mechanical issues that may affect the vehicle's value and performance.

## 5.2 Set a Budget and Stick to It

Before entering the auction, establish a budget for each vehicle you're interested in and stick to it. Consider factors such as the vehicle's market value, your financial constraints, and additional costs such as taxes, fees, and repairs. Avoid getting caught up in the excitement of bidding and exceed your budget, as this can lead to financial strain and regrettable purchases.

## 5.3 Be Strategic in Your Bidding

Develop effective bidding strategies to maximize your chances of winning vehicles at auction:

### 5.3.1 Start Slowly
Begin bidding cautiously and observe the bidding patterns of other participants. Avoid jumping into bidding wars immediately, as this can drive up prices unnecessarily.

### 5.3.2 Bid Confidently
When placing bids, be assertive and confident in your actions. Signal your bids clearly to the auctioneer and maintain a steady pace to keep other bidders on their toes.

### 5.3.3 Know When to Stop
Recognize your limits and be prepared to walk away if bidding exceeds your budget or the vehicle's value. It's better to lose a bid than to overextend yourself financially on a purchase.

## 5.4 Attend Multiple Auctions

To increase your chances of finding the right vehicle at the right price, consider attending multiple auctions and exploring different venues and platforms. Each auction may offer unique inventory, pricing, and bidding dynamics, providing you with diverse options and opportunities.

## 5.5 Learn from Experience

As you gain experience with car auctions, take note of your successes and failures and learn from them. Reflect on your bidding strategies, the vehicles you've purchased, and the outcomes of your purchases. Use this knowledge to refine your approach and improve your results in future auctions.

By following these tips and strategies, you can enhance your bidding skills and increase your likelihood of success at car auctions in Malaysia.

# Chapter 6: Legal and Financial Considerations

In this chapter, we'll discuss the legal and financial aspects of buying vehicles at car auctions in Malaysia, covering important considerations to protect your interests and ensure a smooth transaction process.

## 6.1 Legal Requirements

When purchasing a vehicle at auction, it's essential to comply with legal requirements to transfer ownership and ensure that the transaction is valid and enforceable:

### 6.1.1 Ownership Transfer
After winning a bid at auction, you'll need to complete the necessary paperwork to transfer ownership of the vehicle legally. This typically involves signing a bill of sale, transfer of ownership form, and other documentation required by the relevant authorities.

### 6.1.2 Title Checks
Verify the vehicle's title status and ensure that it is free of liens, encumbrances, or other legal issues that may affect ownership. Conducting title checks before bidding can help you avoid purchasing vehicles with unresolved legal issues.

### 6.1.3 Registration and Taxes
Once you've acquired a vehicle at auction, you'll need to register it with the appropriate authorities and pay any applicable taxes and registration fees. Familiarize yourself with the registration process and tax obligations to ensure compliance with legal requirements.

## 6.2 Financial Considerations

Buying vehicles at auction involves various financial considerations that impact the overall cost of ownership and affordability:

### 6.2.1 Buyer's Premium
Auction houses typically charge a buyer's premium, which is an additional fee added to the winning bid price. The buyer's premium is usually calculated as a percentage of the final bid amount and varies depending on the auction house and the value of the vehicle.

### 6.2.2 Taxes and Duties

In addition to the purchase price and buyer's premium, you'll need to pay taxes and duties on the vehicle, such as sales tax, excise duty, and road tax. These costs can significantly impact the total cost of purchasing a vehicle at auction and should be factored into your budget.

### 6.2.3 Financing Options

Explore financing options available for purchasing vehicles at auction, such as bank loans, financing plans, or installment payments. Evaluate the terms, interest rates, and repayment options to choose the most suitable financing arrangement for your needs.

## 6.3 Legal Protections

To protect your interests when buying vehicles at auction, consider the following legal protections:

### 6.3.1 Auction Terms and Conditions

Review the auction house's terms and conditions carefully before participating in an auction. Pay attention to provisions related to bidding, payment, vehicle inspections, and dispute resolution mechanisms.

### 6.3.2 Warranty and Guarantees

Understand the warranty and guarantee policies offered by the auction house, if any, for vehicles sold at auction. Some auction houses may provide limited warranties or guarantees on certain vehicles, offering recourse in case of defects or issues.

### 6.3.3 Dispute Resolution

Familiarize yourself with the dispute resolution process outlined in the auction house's terms and conditions. In the event of disagreements or disputes arising from a transaction, follow the prescribed procedures to seek resolution through negotiation, mediation, or legal recourse.

By addressing these legal and financial considerations proactively, you can mitigate risks and ensure a secure and legally compliant vehicle purchase at car auctions in Malaysia.

# Chapter 7: Risks and Pitfalls to Avoid

In this chapter, we'll highlight common risks and pitfalls associated with buying vehicles at car auctions in Malaysia, equipping you with the knowledge and awareness to protect yourself and make informed decisions.

## 7.1 Hidden Costs

Buying vehicles at auction involves more than just the winning bid price. Be mindful of the following hidden costs that can impact the total cost of ownership:

### 7.1.1 Buyer's Premium
Auction houses charge a buyer's premium, which is an additional fee added to the winning bid price. The buyer's premium is typically calculated as a percentage of the final bid amount and varies depending on the auction house and the value of the vehicle.

### 7.1.2 Taxes and Duties
In addition to the purchase price and buyer's premium, you'll need to pay taxes and duties on the vehicle, such as sales tax, excise duty, and road tax. These costs can significantly increase the total cost of purchasing a vehicle at auction and should be factored into your budget.

### 7.1.3 Inspection and Repairs
Inspect vehicles thoroughly before bidding to identify any hidden issues or defects that may require repairs. Budget for inspection costs, as well as potential repair expenses, to ensure that you're prepared for any unforeseen repairs that may arise after purchasing the vehicle.

## 7.2 Quality Issues

While car auctions offer the opportunity to find great deals, there's also a risk of purchasing vehicles with quality issues or undisclosed problems. Common quality issues to watch out for include:

### 7.2.1 Mechanical Problems
Some vehicles sold at auction may have underlying mechanical issues, such as engine problems, transmission failures, or suspension issues. Conduct a thorough inspection of the vehicle's mechanical components to identify any potential issues before bidding.

### 7.2.2 Cosmetic Damage
Vehicles at auction may exhibit cosmetic damage, such as dents, scratches, or paint damage. While cosmetic issues may not affect the vehicle's performance, they can detract from its overall appearance and resale value.

### 7.2.3 Salvage Title
Be cautious when purchasing vehicles with salvage titles, as they indicate that the vehicle has been severely damaged or declared a total loss by an insurance company. Salvage vehicles may have undergone extensive repairs and may have hidden structural or safety issues.

## 7.3 Avoiding Scams and Fraud

Unfortunately, car auctions are not immune to scams and fraudulent practices. Protect yourself from scams by following these precautions:

### 7.3.1 Verify Seller Credentials
If purchasing from a private seller or individual, verify their credentials and ensure that they have the legal authority to sell the vehicle. Beware of sellers who refuse to provide documentation or attempt to sell vehicles under suspicious circumstances.

### 7.3.2 Check Vehicle History
Obtain a vehicle history report to check for past accidents, damage, or other issues. Look for discrepancies or inconsistencies in the vehicle's history that may indicate tampering or fraud.

### 7.3.3 Beware of Unrealistic Deals
Exercise caution when encountering deals that seem too good to be true. Scammers may lure unsuspecting buyers with unrealistically low prices or promises of guaranteed returns. Conduct thorough research and use common sense to avoid falling victim to scams.

## 7.4 Lack of Warranty or Recourse

Unlike purchases from dealerships, vehicles bought at auction may not come with warranties or guarantees. As such, buyers assume the risk of any defects or issues discovered after the sale. To mitigate this risk:

### 7.4.1 Inspect Vehicles Thoroughly
Prior to bidding, thoroughly inspect vehicles for any signs of damage, wear, or mechanical issues. Take note of any concerns and factor them into your decision-making process.

### 7.4.2 Consider Professional Inspection
If you're unsure about a vehicle's condition, consider hiring a qualified mechanic or automotive expert to conduct a comprehensive inspection. A professional inspection can provide valuable insights and identify potential issues that may not be apparent to the untrained eye.

### 7.4.3 Know Your Rights
Familiarize yourself with consumer protection laws and regulations governing vehicle purchases in Malaysia. While auction purchases may not always come with warranties, you may still have legal recourse in cases of misrepresentation, fraud, or breach of contract.

By being vigilant and proactive, you can minimize the risks and pitfalls associated with buying vehicles at car auctions in Malaysia.

# Chapter 8: Case Studies and Success Stories

In this chapter, we'll explore real-life case studies and success stories of individuals who have navigated the car auction market in Malaysia successfully. These stories provide valuable insights and inspiration for aspiring auction buyers.

## 8.1 Case Study: Adam's Auction Adventure

Adam, a car enthusiast from Kuala Lumpur, had always dreamed of owning a classic sports car. However, he was on a tight budget and wasn't sure where to start. Upon learning about car auctions in Malaysia, Adam decided to explore his options and see if he could find his dream car at an affordable price.

Adam began his auction adventure by researching different auction houses and online platforms, familiarizing himself with their inventory and bidding processes. He attended several auctions to get a feel for the atmosphere and observe bidding dynamics.

After months of searching, Adam finally spotted his dream car—a vintage Porsche 911—in an online auction. With careful research and preparation, Adam placed a strategic bid and won the auction, securing the car of his dreams at a fraction of its market value.

Adam's success story demonstrates the importance of patience, perseverance, and strategic bidding in the car auction market. By staying informed and taking calculated risks, Adam was able to turn his dream into reality and acquire a coveted classic car.

## 8.2 Success Story: Sarah's Smart Investment

Sarah, a young professional from Penang, was in the market for a reliable and affordable vehicle to commute to work. Instead of purchasing a brand-new car from a dealership, Sarah decided to explore the option of buying a used car at auction.

Sarah conducted extensive research on different auction platforms and attended several auctions to familiarize herself with the process. She set a strict budget and carefully inspected each vehicle she was interested in, paying close attention to their condition and maintenance history.

At one auction, Sarah came across a well-maintained Toyota Vios with low mileage and a clean service record. With confidence in her research and inspection, Sarah placed a competitive bid and successfully won the auction, securing a reliable car at a significantly lower price than buying from a dealership.

Sarah's smart investment demonstrates the value of buying used cars at auction as an affordable and practical alternative to purchasing new vehicles. By leveraging her knowledge and conducting thorough research, Sarah was able to make a wise investment and find a quality car that met her needs and budget.

These case studies and success stories illustrate the diverse opportunities and benefits of participating in car auctions in Malaysia. Whether you're a car enthusiast searching for a classic car or a budget-conscious buyer looking for a reliable vehicle, car auctions offer a wealth of options and possibilities.

# Chapter 9: Future Outlook and Trends

In this chapter, we'll explore the future outlook and emerging trends shaping the car auction market in Malaysia. From technological advancements to shifting consumer preferences, these trends offer insights into the evolving landscape of automotive auctions.

## 9.1 Emerging Technologies

Advancements in technology are revolutionizing the car auction industry, offering new opportunities for buyers and sellers alike:

### 9.1.1 Online Auction Platforms
The popularity of online auction platforms continues to grow, providing buyers with greater convenience and accessibility. Expect to see further innovations in online bidding systems, virtual inspections, and digital payment solutions.

### 9.1.2 Artificial Intelligence and Data Analytics
Auction houses are increasingly leveraging artificial intelligence and data analytics to improve pricing strategies, predict market trends, and enhance the auction experience. AI-powered tools can analyze vast amounts of data to provide valuable insights and optimize decision-making processes.

### 9.1.3 Virtual Reality and Augmented Reality
Virtual reality and augmented reality technologies are being used to create immersive auction experiences, allowing buyers to view and inspect vehicles in a virtual environment. These technologies offer new opportunities for remote participation and enhanced visualization of auction inventory.

## 9.2 Sustainable Practices

As environmental concerns continue to gain traction, expect to see a greater emphasis on sustainability and eco-friendly practices in the car auction industry:

### 9.2.1 Electric and Hybrid Vehicles
The demand for electric and hybrid vehicles is on the rise, driven by concerns about air pollution and climate change. Auctions will increasingly feature electric and hybrid models, as well as incentives for buyers to adopt environmentally friendly vehicles.

### 9.2.2 Green Initiatives
Auction houses are implementing green initiatives to reduce their environmental footprint, such as recycling, energy efficiency measures, and eco-friendly transportation options. By embracing sustainable practices, auction houses can demonstrate their commitment to environmental stewardship and attract environmentally conscious buyers.

### 9.2.3 Emission Standards Compliance
With stricter regulations on vehicle emissions, auction houses will prioritize vehicles that meet or exceed emission standards. Buyers can expect greater transparency regarding vehicles' emission levels and compliance with regulatory requirements.

## 9.3 Shift in Consumer Preferences

Changing consumer preferences are influencing the types of vehicles available at auctions and the way auctions are conducted:

### 9.3.1 Demand for Connected Cars
Consumers are increasingly seeking vehicles equipped with advanced technology features, such as connectivity, navigation systems, and driver assistance technologies. Auctions will cater to this demand by offering a greater selection of connected cars with modern amenities.

### 9.3.2 Flexible Ownership Models
The rise of shared mobility and alternative ownership models, such as car-sharing and subscription services, is reshaping the automotive industry. Auctions may feature vehicles from fleet operators and rental companies, reflecting the growing popularity of shared mobility solutions.

### 9.3.3 Online Participation
The convenience of online bidding and virtual auctions is attracting more buyers to participate remotely. Expect to see continued growth in online auction platforms and digital auction experiences, offering buyers greater flexibility and accessibility.

## 9.4 Market Expansion

The car auction market in Malaysia is poised for further expansion, driven by economic growth, urbanization, and increased consumer demand:

### 9.4.1 Regional Integration
Malaysia's strategic location in Southeast Asia positions it as a hub for regional automotive trade and commerce. Auction houses may collaborate with international partners to expand their reach and access to a broader pool of buyers and sellers.

### 9.4.2 Digital Transformation
The ongoing digital transformation of the automotive industry will continue to shape the car auction market in Malaysia. Auction houses will invest in digital infrastructure, cybersecurity, and online marketing strategies to stay competitive in the digital age.

### 9.4.3 Diversity of Inventory
Buyers can expect to see a greater diversity of inventory at auctions, including electric vehicles, autonomous vehicles, and mobility solutions. Auctions will adapt to changing consumer preferences and market trends, offering innovative and sustainable mobility solutions.

As the car auction market in Malaysia evolves, opportunities abound for buyers to find quality vehicles at competitive prices and for sellers to reach a wider audience. By staying informed about emerging trends and embracing technological advancements, participants can navigate the dynamic landscape of automotive auctions with confidence and success.

# Chapter 10: Additional Resources and Glossary

In this final chapter, we'll provide readers with valuable additional resources to further their understanding of car auctions in Malaysia. Additionally, we'll include a glossary of common auction terms to help readers navigate the auction process more confidently.

## 10.1 Additional Resources

To continue your journey into the world of car auctions in Malaysia, consider exploring the following additional resources:

### 10.1.1 Online Auction Platforms
Visit reputable online auction platforms and websites specializing in car auctions in Malaysia. These platforms often provide valuable information, auction listings, and bidding opportunities. The following are some examples of online auction platforms for your reference.

- e-biddi.com
- bidonline.my
- ksljb.my

### 10.1.2 Auction Houses
Reach out to local auction houses and inquire about their upcoming auctions, registration processes, and services offered. Many auction houses host regular events and provide resources for buyers and sellers. Examples of auction houses as below.

- Pickles Asia Sdn. Bhd. (pickles.my)
- Ng Chan Mau & Co Sdn. Bhd. (ngchanmau.com)
- Inter Pacific Auto Auction Sdn. Bhd. (ipaa-ebid.com)

### 10.1.3 Automotive Forums and Communities
Join online forums and communities dedicated to car enthusiasts and auction participants. Engage with fellow members, ask questions, and share experiences to gain insights and tips from experienced auction attendees. Some examples as below.

### 10.1.4 Automotive Publications
Subscribe to automotive magazines, blogs, and publications that cover car auctions, market trends, and industry news. These sources often provide in-depth analysis, expert opinions, and insider perspectives on the automotive auction market. Some examples as below.

### 10.1.5 Government Websites
Visit government websites, such as the Royal Malaysian Customs Department and the Road Transport Department (JPJ), for information on government auctions, regulations, and procedures for purchasing seized or surplus vehicles.

## 10.2 Glossary of Auction Terms

To help readers familiarize themselves with common auction terminology, here is a glossary of terms frequently encountered in car auctions:

**Auctioneer**
The person responsible for conducting the auction, announcing bids, and facilitating the bidding process.

**Bid**
An offer or proposal to purchase a vehicle at a specific price during the auction.

**Buyer's Premium**
An additional fee charged to the buyer on top of the winning bid price, typically calculated as a percentage of the final bid amount.

**Reserve Price**
The minimum price set by the seller that must be met or exceeded for the vehicle to be sold at auction.

**Lot**
A group or collection of vehicles offered for sale at the auction.

**Hammer Price**
The final bid price at which the vehicle is sold, determined by the auctioneer's hammer or gavel.

**Reserve Not Met**
Indicates that the reserve price set by the seller has not been reached, and the vehicle will not be sold unless a higher bid is received.

**Absentee Bid**
A bid placed by a buyer who is unable to attend the auction in person, typically submitted in advance or through a proxy bidder.

**Buyer's Fee**
A fee charged to the buyer in addition to the winning bid price, similar to a buyer's premium.

**Title**
Legal documentation proving ownership of the vehicle, required for transferring ownership to the buyer.

These resources and glossary terms aim to empower readers with the knowledge and tools they need to navigate car auctions in Malaysia confidently.

## Conclusion

In conclusion, car auctions in Malaysia offer a wealth of opportunities for buyers and sellers alike. From the thrill of competitive bidding to the satisfaction of finding the perfect vehicle, auctions provide a unique and dynamic marketplace for automotive enthusiasts and savvy shoppers.

By understanding the auction process, conducting thorough research, and adopting effective bidding strategies, buyers can navigate the complexities of car auctions with confidence and increase their chances of success. Whether you're searching for a classic car, a reliable daily driver, or a commercial vehicle for your business, car auctions offer a diverse selection of vehicles to suit every need and budget.

As the automotive industry continues to evolve, so too will the car auction market in Malaysia. By staying informed about emerging trends, embracing technological advancements, and adhering to best practices, participants can position themselves for success in this exciting and ever-changing industry.

Whether you're a seasoned auction veteran or a first-time bidder, I hope this ebook has provided valuable insights and practical tips to enhance your auction experience. Remember to approach auctions with patience, diligence, and a sense of adventure, and you'll be well on your way to finding your next dream car at a car auction in Malaysia.

Happy bidding!

# Frequently Asked Questions (FAQ)

1. **What are car auctions, and how do they work in Malaysia?**
   Car auctions in Malaysia are events where vehicles are sold to the highest bidder. These auctions are usually conducted by auction houses or online platforms approved by relevant authorities. Vehicles are typically sourced from various channels, including repossessed vehicles, trade-ins, or fleet disposals.

2. **Who can participate in car auctions in Malaysia?**
   Generally, anyone with the necessary documentation and registration can participate in car auctions in Malaysia. This includes individuals, dealerships, and businesses. However, some auctions may have specific eligibility criteria or require pre-registration.

3. **What types of vehicles are typically available at car auctions in Malaysia?**
   Car auctions in Malaysia offer a wide range of vehicles, including used cars, repossessed vehicles, luxury cars, commercial vehicles, and even salvage vehicles. The availability of specific types of vehicles may vary depending on the auction house or platform.

4. **How can I register for a car auction in Malaysia?**
   Registration processes may differ between auction houses or platforms. Generally, you'll need to provide identification documents, proof of address, and possibly a registration fee. Online platforms may require additional steps for account creation and verification.

5. **What are the benefits of buying a car at an auction in Malaysia compared to traditional methods?**
   Buying a car at auction in Malaysia can offer potential cost savings compared to buying from dealerships or private sellers. Additionally, auctions provide a wide selection of vehicles and may offer opportunities to find unique or rare models.

6. **What are some common mistakes to avoid when participating in car auctions in Malaysia?**
   Common mistakes include overbidding, not inspecting vehicles thoroughly, neglecting to set a budget, and not understanding auction rules and procedures. It's essential to research and prepare adequately before participating in an auction.

7. **How do I assess the condition of a vehicle before bidding at an auction in Malaysia?**
   It's crucial to inspect vehicles thoroughly before bidding. This may include checking the exterior, interior, engine condition, mileage, service history, and conducting a test drive if possible. Some auctions may provide inspection reports or allow pre-auction inspections.

8. **What documents do I need to bring to a car auction in Malaysia?**
   Required documents typically include identification (such as IC or passport), proof of address, and any registration or membership documents provided by the auction house or platform.

9. **What payment methods are accepted at car auctions in Malaysia?**
   Payment methods may vary but commonly include cash, cashier's checks, bank drafts, or online bank transfers. It's essential to confirm accepted payment methods with the auction organizer beforehand.

10. **Are there any hidden fees or charges associated with purchasing a car at auction in Malaysia?**
    While auction houses may charge buyer's premiums or administrative fees, these are usually transparent and disclosed upfront. It's essential to review the auction terms and conditions to understand all potential fees associated with purchasing a vehicle.

11. **What happens if I win a bid at a car auction in Malaysia?**
    If you win a bid at a car auction in Malaysia, you're typically required to complete the purchase by paying the final bid amount along with any applicable fees. The auction house will provide instructions for payment and vehicle pickup or delivery.

12. **Can I inspect the vehicles before the auction begins in Malaysia?**
    Many auctions allow prospective buyers to inspect vehicles before the auction starts. This gives buyers an opportunity to assess the condition of the vehicles and make informed bidding decisions. Some auctions may also provide detailed vehicle descriptions or inspection reports.

13. **What are the legal obligations and responsibilities of buyers at car auctions in Malaysia?**
Buyers are typically expected to adhere to the auction's terms and conditions, including completing the purchase if they win a bid. It's essential to understand the legal implications of participating in an auction and to comply with all relevant laws and regulations.

14. **Are there any warranties or guarantees on vehicles purchased at auction in Malaysia?**
Vehicles sold at auction in Malaysia are usually sold on an "as-is, where-is" basis, meaning there are typically no warranties or guarantees provided. Buyers should inspect vehicles thoroughly and understand that they are responsible for any repairs or issues after purchase.

15. **Can I sell a car I purchased at auction in Malaysia?**
Yes, you can sell a car purchased at auction in Malaysia. However, you'll need to transfer ownership properly and ensure all necessary documentation is completed. Depending on the condition and market demand, you may sell the vehicle privately or through another auction.

16. **What are the differences between online and physical car auctions in Malaysia?**
Online auctions allow participants to bid on vehicles remotely, while physical auctions require attendance at a specific location. Online auctions may offer convenience and accessibility, while physical auctions provide the opportunity for in-person vehicle inspection and networking.

17. **Are there any special considerations for international buyers participating in car auctions in Malaysia?**
International buyers may need to consider factors such as import regulations, taxes, and shipping costs when purchasing vehicles at auction in Malaysia. It's advisable to research these considerations beforehand and consult with relevant authorities or professionals if necessary.

18. **How do I transport a vehicle purchased at auction in Malaysia?**
After purchasing a vehicle at auction in Malaysia, you'll need to arrange for transportation to your desired location. This may involve hiring a professional vehicle transporter or arranging for self-pickup using appropriate transportation equipment.

19. **What is Puspakom inspection, and why is it necessary after winning a bid at a car auction in Malaysia?**
    Puspakom inspection, conducted by Puspakom (Pusat Pemeriksaan Kenderaan Berkomputer), is a mandatory vehicle inspection required for all vehicle transfers in Malaysia. It ensures the vehicle's roadworthiness and compliance with safety and environmental standards.

20. **When should I schedule the Puspakom inspection after winning a bid at a car auction in Malaysia?**
    It's advisable to schedule the Puspakom inspection as soon as possible after winning the bid to expedite the process of transferring ownership. Delays in scheduling the inspection may prolong the overall ownership transfer process.

21. **What documents do I need for the Puspakom inspection after winning a bid at a car auction in Malaysia?**
    Documents required for the Puspakom inspection typically include the vehicle registration card (Grant), if any, the original sales invoice or auction receipt, and your identification documents (IC or passport).

22. **How do I schedule a Puspakom inspection after winning a bid at a car auction in Malaysia?**
    You can schedule a Puspakom inspection by contacting Puspakom directly or through their online appointment booking system. Ensure you have all necessary documents and payment ready when scheduling the inspection.

23. **What happens during the Puspakom inspection after winning a bid at a car auction in Malaysia?**
    During the Puspakom inspection, the vehicle will undergo various checks to assess its roadworthiness, including inspections of the chassis, engine, brakes, lights, and emissions. Once the vehicle passes the inspection, you'll receive a Puspakom inspection certificate.

24. **After passing the Puspakom inspection, what are the next steps for transferring ownership with JPJ (Jabatan Pengangkutan Jalan)?**
After passing the Puspakom inspection, you'll need to proceed with the transfer of ownership at the JPJ. This involves submitting the necessary documents and completing the ownership transfer process with the JPJ.

25. **What documents do I need for the JPJ change of ownership process after winning a bid at a car auction in Malaysia?**
Required documents for the JPJ change of ownership process typically include the Puspakom inspection certificate, the vehicle registration card (Grant), if any, your identification documents (IC or passport), and any other relevant documents provided by the auction house.

26. **Are there any fees involved in the Puspakom inspection and JPJ change of ownership process after winning a bid at a car auction in Malaysia?**
Yes, there are fees associated with both the Puspakom inspection and JPJ change of ownership process. These fees may vary depending on the type of vehicle, location, and specific services required. It's essential to inquire about the applicable fees beforehand and prepare accordingly.

27. **What happens if the vehicle fails the Puspakom inspection after winning a bid at a car auction in Malaysia?**
If the vehicle fails the Puspakom inspection, you'll need to address the identified issues to bring the vehicle into compliance with the required standards. Depending on the nature of the failures, this may involve repairing or replacing certain components, addressing safety concerns, or rectifying emissions issues. Once the necessary repairs are completed, you can schedule a re-inspection with Puspakom to verify compliance.

28. **What are the consequences of not completing the Puspakom inspection after winning a bid at a car auction in Malaysia?**
Failing to complete the Puspakom inspection within the required timeframe can result in delays in the ownership transfer process and may also lead to legal implications. It's essential to adhere to the inspection requirements and promptly schedule the inspection to avoid any potential penalties or complications.

**29. Is it possible to transfer ownership of a vehicle without undergoing the Puspakom inspection after winning a bid at a car auction in Malaysia?**

No, the Puspakom inspection is mandatory for all vehicle transfers in Malaysia, including those obtained through auctions. Failure to comply with this requirement can result in the rejection of the ownership transfer application by the JPJ. It's essential to complete the inspection as per the regulatory requirements to facilitate a smooth ownership transfer process.

www.ingramcontent.com/pod-product-compliance
Lightning Source LLC
Chambersburg PA
CBHW070956220526
45471CB00007B/3049